Gone Forever!
Velociraptor

Rupert Matthews

Heinemann Library
Chicago, Illinois

Customer Service 888-454-2279
Visit our website at www.heinemannlibrary.com

Designed by Ron Kamen and Paul Davies and Associates
Illustrations by James Field of Simon Girling and Associates
Photo Research by Rebecca Sodergren and Ginny Stroud-Lewis
Originated by Ambassador Litho Ltd.
Printed and bound in China by South China Printing Company

07 06 05 04
10 9 8 7 6 5 4 3 2

Library of Congress Cataloging-in-Publication Data
Matthews, Rupert.
  Velociraptor / Rupert Matthews.
      p. cm. -- (Gone forever!)
Summary: Describes what has been learned about the physical features, behavior, and surroundings of the long-extinct velociraptor.
Includes bibliographical references and index.
  ISBN 1-4034-3659-2 (hardcover) -- ISBN 1-4034-3670-3 (pbk.)
  1. Velociraptor--Juvenile literature. [1. Velociraptor. 2. Dinosaurs.] I. Title.
  QE862.S3.M3328 2003
  567.912--dc22

                          2003012299

Acknowledgments
The author and publishers are grateful to the following for permission to reproduce copyright material: pp. 12, 18, 20, 22, 24 American Museum of Natural History; p. 6 Robert Campbell/Sygma/Corbis; p. 10 Layne Kennedy/Corbis; pp. 8, 14 Geoscience Features; pp. 4, 26 Natural History Museum, London; p. 16 Oregon State University.
Cover photograph reproduced with permission of the American Museum of Natural History.

Special thanks to Dr. Peter Makovicky of the Chicago Field Museum for his review of this book.

Some words are shown in bold, **like this.** You can find out what they mean by looking in the glossary.

Contents

Gone Forever!

Some animals are **extinct.** This means that they have all died and none are left alive. Scientists called **paleontologists** study the **fossils** of these animals. They find out about the animals and how they lived.

Velociraptor was a **dinosaur** that is now
extinct. It lived about 80 million years ago
in central Asia. It hunted and killed other
dinosaurs. Then it ate them.

Velociraptor's Hunting Grounds

Scientists called **geologists** study the rocks where **fossils** are found. The geologists can learn about the places where **dinosaurs** lived by looking at the rocks.

Velociraptor lived in places that were fairly dry
and warm. Some trees grew there. Most of the
land was covered by desert. But the land was
dotted here and there with scrubby bushes and
other short plants.

Plants

Paleontologists have found **fossils** of plants in the same rocks as Velociraptor fossils. These fossils show what types of plants grew in the land of Velociraptor. A few of these plants may have had bright, colorful flowers.

fossil of a plant

8

Some of the plants that grew at the time of Velociraptor were flowering bushes. In some places, these were like the modern trees called **magnolias.** Other plants were different from plants that grow today. Along with bushes, a few **fir** and pine trees grew in the dry land.

9

Living with Velociraptor

Many other types of animals lived alongside Velociraptor. Some of these were birds. Only a few bird **fossils** from the time of Velociraptor have survived. This fossil of a feather is from many millions of years later.

Birds probably lived among the bushes. Some ate the new types of **insects** that appeared at this time. These insects included butterflies and bees, which fed on the flowers. Flying **reptiles** called **pterosaurs** glided high in the skies.

What Was Velociraptor?

Paleontologists have studied the **fossils** of Velociraptor. They use the fossils to find out what kind of animal Velociraptor was. The teeth show what kind of food Velociraptor ate. The **limbs** show how it got its food.

12

Velociraptor was a hunter, or **predator.** It killed and ate other **dinosaurs.** It was about as long as a grown man. It had sharp claws and teeth. It used its claws and teeth to kill other dinosaurs.

Velociraptor Nests

Scientists have found **fossils** of **dinosaur** eggs like the ones below. This nest belonged to a dinosaur called Oviraptor. The Oviraptor laid its eggs in a circle with the narrow end down in the nest. Scientists think that Velociraptor laid its eggs this way, too.

Oviraptor eggs

The mother Velociraptor probably stayed near
the nest. She would protect the eggs from any
animals that tried to eat them. The mother made
sure the eggs stayed warm. She might even have
sat on the nest.

15

Growing Up

Paleontologists have found **fossils** of young **dinosaurs** that were like Velociraptor. They can learn about Velociraptor by studying these fossils. They show that baby Velociraptors may have been hunters. But they were weaker than grown-ups and had smaller claws.

fossil of a baby Scipionyx dinosaur

Baby Velociraptors were too small to hunt other
dinosaurs. They probably ate **lizards** and other
small animals. They may even have hunted **insects**
such as beetles. As they grew older, Velociraptors
began to kill larger animals.

17

Speedy Hunters

Velociraptor had strong back legs and a long, stiff tail. **Fossils** show that these parts were connected to powerful hip **muscles.** These muscles gave Velociraptor the power to run quickly and change direction suddenly.

This fossil is Deinonychus, a dinosaur like Velociraptor.

Paleontologists believe that Velociraptor hunted its **prey** by dashing between bushes and shrubs. Its long legs and light weight meant that it was very fast. Scientists also think that Velociraptors hunted in **packs.** The name *Velociraptor* means "fast hunter."

Killer claws!

Velociraptor's back feet were not like those of other **dinosaurs.** The second toe of each foot had a huge, curved claw.

The claw was very sharp. A Velociraptor could flick its toe forward with great force. The claw stabbed into Velociraptor's **prey.**

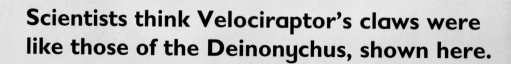

Scientists think Velociraptor's claws were like those of the Deinonychus, shown here.

20

Paleontologists think that Velociraptor hunted other dinosaurs. It slashed them with its large claws. It may have jumped onto another dinosaur and killed it with one mighty kick! Here, a Velociraptor is jumping on a Protoceratops.

21

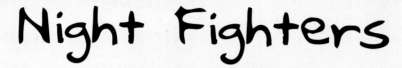

Night Fighters

The **fossil** skulls of Velociraptor shows it had large eyes. Other animals with large eyes can see well in dim light. **Paleontologists** think Velociraptor may have been able to see well at night.

Velociraptor skull

Velociraptor may have hunted by moonlight
or in the dim light of dusk. Other **dinosaurs**
probably hid from Velociraptor in the shadows.

Food for Velociraptor

Paleontologists have found one Velociraptor **fossil** with its claws wrapped around the **frill** of a **dinosaur** called Protoceratops. Protoceratops ate plants. Scientists believe that Protoceratops was one of the Velociraptor's favorite **prey.**

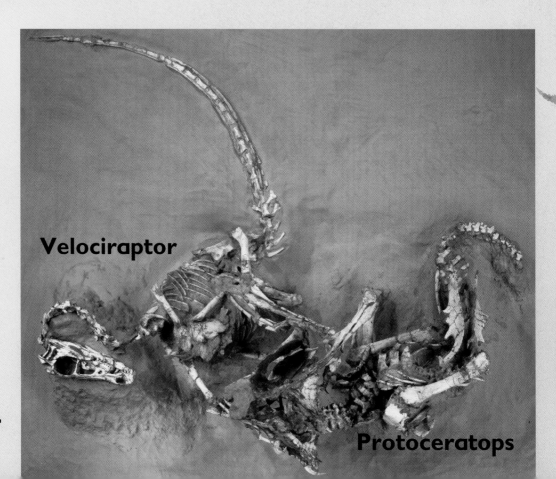

Velociraptor

Protoceratops

Protoceratops walked on all four legs. It could hide
from Velociraptor among the bushes. Protoceratops
had a powerful **beak** for eating tough plants. It
could use its beak to bite at Velociraptor.

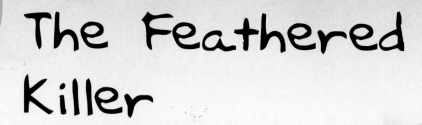

The Feathered Killer

Paleontologists have found some very good **fossils** of small hunting **dinosaurs.** The dinosaurs were covered with feathers. These fossils show that birds are related to dinosaurs.

feathers

Most paleontologists think that Velociraptor had feathers, too. It may have had short feathers on its body to keep it warm, with longer feathers on its tail and arms. The feathers may have been very colorful.

27

Where Did Velociraptor Live?

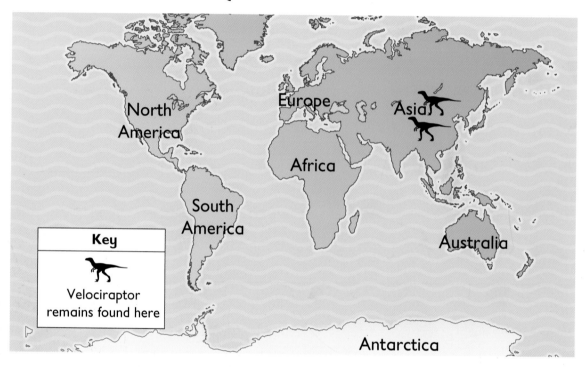

Paleontolgists have found Velociraptor **fossils** in Asia. They were discovered in the Gobi Desert, which covers parts of China and Mongolia.

When Did Velociraptor Live?

Velociraptor lived in the Age of **Dinosaurs.**
Scientists call this the Mesozoic Era. Velociraptor
lived between 80 and 77 million years ago. This
was near the end of what scientists call the
Cretaceous Period.

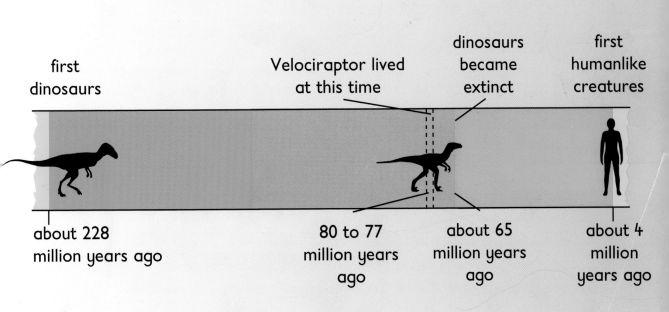

first
dinosaurs

Velociraptor lived
at this time

dinosaurs
became
extinct

first
humanlike
creatures

about 228
million years ago

80 to 77
million years
ago

about 65
million years
ago

about 4
million
years ago

Fact File

Velociraptor	
Length:	up to 6 $\frac{1}{2}$ feet (2 meters)
Height:	up to 5 feet (1.5 meters)
Weight:	about 33 pounds (15 kilograms)
Time:	Late Cretaceous Period, about 80 million years ago
Place:	Central Asia

How to Say It

Velociraptor—vuh-los-ah-rap-tur
Cretaceaus—krih-tay-shuhs
dinosaur—dine-ah-sor
paleontologist—pay-lee-uhn-tahl-uh-jist
Protoceratops—proh-toh-sair-ah-tops
pterosaur—tair-ah-sor

Glossary

beak hard, horny covering on jaws used in place of teeth

dinosaur reptile that lived on Earth between 228 and 65 million years ago. Dinosaurs are extinct.

extinct word that describes plants and animals that once lived on Earth but have all died out

fir tree that keeps its leaves all year. The leaves are skinny and always green.

fossil remains of a plant or animal, usually found in rocks

frill fringe of bone at the back of some dinosaurs' heads. Protoceratops and Triceratops had frills.

geologist scientist who studies rocks

hatch break out of an egg

insect small animal with six legs

limb arm or leg

lizard type of reptile that usually has a big body and tail, four legs, and eyelids that move

magnolia shrub or tree with woody branches, dark green leaves, and white or pink flowers.

muscle part of an animal's body that makes it move

pack group of animals that live and hunt together

paleontologist scientist who studies fossils to learn about extinct animals, such as dinosaurs

predator animal that hunts other animals for food

prey animal that is hunted and eaten by another animal

pterosaur flying reptile that lived at the same time as the dinosaurs. They looked kind of like modern bats but were not related. There were several different types of pterosaurs.

reptile cold-blooded animal with scaly skin. Snakes, lizards, dinosaurs, and crocodiles are all reptiles.

More Books to Read

Cohen, Daniel. *Velociraptor*. Mankato, Minn.: Capstone Press, 2000.

Landau, Elaina. *Velociraptor*. New York: Children's Press, 1999.

Wilkes, Angela. *Big Book of Dinosaurs*. New York: Dorling Kindersley, 1994.

Index